DISCOVERING MATH

SUBTRACTION

ALISON WELLS

■

ART BY RICHARD MACCABE

BENCHMARK BOOKS

MARSHALL CAVENDISH
NEW YORK

Benchmark Books
Marshall Cavendish Corporation
99 White Plains Road
Tarrytown, New York 10591-9001

©Marshall Cavendish Corporation, 1996

Series created by Blackbirch Graphics, Inc.

Library of Congress Cataloging-in-Publication Data

Wells, Alison
    Subtraction / by Alison Wells; illustrated by Richard Maccabe.
        p.   cm. — (Discovering math)
    Includes index.
    ISBN 0-7614-0594-1 (lib. bdg.)
    1. Subtraction — Juvenile literature. 2. Mathematical recreations — Juvenile literature. [1. Subtraction. 2. Mathematical recreations.] I. Maccabe, Richard, ill. II. Title. III. Series.
QA115.W45   1995
513.2'12—dc20

95-13573
CIP
AC

Contents

Popcorn Pitch	4
Card Smart	5
Checkers Challenge	6
The Gremlin's Gold	8
It's Nothing, Really!	10
Noodle Numbers	11
The Tortoise, the Hare, and...	12
Red Alert	14
Zero to Sixty	16
Shopping Spree	18
Pocket Money	20
Gallons of Guppies	21
And the Answer Is...	22
Code Breaking	24
A-Maze-ing 10,000	26
Answers	27
Glossary	31
Index	32

Popcorn Pitch

Here's a great trick to play the next time someone at your house makes popcorn. First, tell your family that you have amazing powers. Explain that you will be able to tell how many pieces of popcorn are in a bag—*without looking inside.* They will probably want you to prove it. Here's how:

• Get a big grocery bag and put it against a wall.

• Stand five giant steps away from the bag.

• Take fifteen pieces of popcorn and toss them, one at a time, into a bag.

• Count the number of pieces that miss the bag. Take away the number that missed from the fifteen you started with. The remainder are in the bag.

• Make your prediction to your family. Then have someone look in the bag to see if you were right. Ta da!

• Prove that you can do this amazing trick again and again. Each time, you will be able to predict correctly the number of pieces of popcorn that are in the bag.

If someone says, "That's truly amazing," you can say, "No. That's subtraction."

Don't forget to eat the popcorn in the bag, too.

Card Smart

You really will have to be "Card Smart" to figure out these card puzzles. Get a deck of cards and deal out the "hands" you see.

• Add up the numbers shown on the cards in each hand.

• Take away one card from each hand (and subtract its value) so that the sum of the two remaining cards for all four hands is the same number. What's the number?

Now try this set of hands.

• What's the magic number?

• Can you make up your own hand of spades to fit the puzzle?

Checkers Challenge

Have you ever played Checkers? Even if you haven't, here's a Checkers challenge to test your wits.

Here are some pointers before you start. There are two play-ers—Black and Red. Each tries to take the other player's check-ers. The player who manages to take all the other player's pieces wins the game. At the beginning of a game, the checkerboard looks like this:

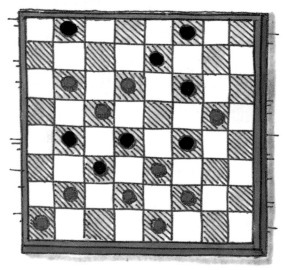

Now let's imagine a game has begun. Use bottle caps and coins to act out the game. You will need twelve of each.

Who is ahead? How far ahead?
How do you know?

The game continues. Each player has now taken several more pieces. Here are the pieces that have been taken:

• How many checkers does Red have left on the board?

• How many checkers does Black have left on the board?

• How many more checkers on the board does Red have than Black?

• How many more checkers does Black have to take in order to have taken the same number as Red?

The Gremlin's Gold

Here's a game for two to four players. You will need two paper clips, pencils, a large jar lid, a ruler, and paper to make spinners like these.

Here's how the game goes. A gremlin found fifty pieces of gold. He hurried to hide them in his cave, but he dropped some along the way.

Your goal is to get as many gold pieces as you can. You can get gold by being first to land on squares with gold or by getting to the cave first. Each player will need a marker to move. Put coins, bottle caps, or bits of paper on the squares and in the cave to represent the gold as shown on the board.

This is where it gets tricky! This could be 18-9 or 10-9 or 18-2 or 10-2.

• Spin to see who goes first. The player with the highest spin on the higher numbers spinner goes first.

• Spin both spinners. Subtract one of the numbers on the smaller numbers spinner from one of the numbers on the larger numbers spinner. This tells you how many squares to move. Each time you spin, there are four possible moves. Pick the one that helps you land on gold, or avoid losing gold.

8

• If you are the first to land on a square with gold, you get to take it. If you land on a "lose gold" square, you must give up the required gold (if you have it) and put it on the square. The next player to land there can take it. To get the gold in the gremlin's cave, your move must be exact, not over. Good luck!

It's Nothing, Really!

Take any four numbers. For example, try these:

Subtract each number from the one next to it. Then subtract the numbers at the beginning and end of the row.

Hint: Always subtract the smaller number from the larger number.

Write your answers in a row below the numbers you started with, like this:

It's nothing. Really!

Keep subtracting in the same way until you can go no further.

• How many rows did you end up with?

• What happened in the last two rows?

Try this trick with four different numbers. Does it work? Do it again and amaze your friends.

Noodle Numbers

How well do you know your noodles? Do you know, for example, that people in Italy have been eating pasta (another name for noodles) for more than 700 years? And do you know the names of the kinds of pasta you see here? Which is lasagna (lu-SAHN-yu) and which is linguini (lin-GWEE-nee)?

If you guessed that the fat pasta is lasagna, you're right!

Now, you'll need some lasagna and linguini for this activity. If you can't find the right noodles, cut paper strips to use instead.

Let's say a ⬭ stands for a ten and a / stands for a one. Can you tell what numbers these noodles stand for?

Now try to solve these pasta problems using noodle numbers.

• Draw a picture of your noodle answers.

The Tortoise, the Hare, and...

In the story of the tortoise and the hare, the moral was "slow but steady wins the race." But have you ever wondered who's really faster than whom in the animal kingdom? Some animals might surprise you!

• Use the clues to figure out the speed of each of the animals in miles per hour.

• Rank the animals from 1 to 10 (fastest to slowest).

• Stump your friends. See if they can put the animals in the right order.

A giant tortoise is more than 10 miles per hour slower than a pig.

A rabbit's pace is 35 miles per hour slower than a cheetah's.

A pig is 2 miles per hour faster than a chicken.

The cheetah is the fastest land animal. It can run at speeds of 70 miles per hour.

A lion can run 15 miles per hour faster than a rabbit.

A cat is 20 miles per hour slower than a lion.

A chicken is 21 miles per hour slower than a cat.

A coyote runs 7 miles per hour slower than a lion.

A giraffe is 11 miles per hour slower than a coyote.

A human runs between 7 and 8 miles per hour slower than a rabbit.

13

Tally charts make it easy to keep track of things. Each / is one. Each //// is five.

Red Alert

What's your favorite color? How popular do you think it is? Here's a way to find out.

Let's say your favorite color is red. You could take a survey to see how many people are wearing red. If you made a chart of your results, here's what it might look like:

Red	No Red
//// //// //// //	//// //// //// //// //// //// ///

• How many people wore red? How many did not? Which group was larger? How much larger?

Are you ready to do a survey of your own? Choose any color you want. Make a chart like the one on page 14. Now all you need is a place where you can watch and tally. A library, the school cafeteria, or a park bench might work well. Try to count at least fifty people.

• How many people did you count? How many wore your favorite color? How many did not? Which group was larger? How much larger?

If you want, tally with a friend whose favorite color is different from yours. Make sure you record the same people.

• Compare your results. How many wore your favorite color? How many wore your friend's favorite? How many wore neither? Which group is larger? How much larger?

WALK

Zero to Sixty

How high is 60 inches? Let's see how close you can come. You will need a friend and a measuring tape at least 60 inches long to take on this challenge.

Go head to head. Each of you try to build a tower as close to 60 inches high as you can.

• Collect objects that you think, when stacked, will measure about 60 inches.

• Stack your stuff. If your tower keeps toppling, try putting it in a corner.

• Measure each stack. How much over or under 60 inches is each stack? Whose stack is closer to 60 inches? How much closer?

• Try to get closer to 60 inches by replacing one of your objects with a different one.

• Measure again. Now how much over or under 60 inches is each stack? Whose stack is closer to 60 inches? How much closer?

• Keep going. Replace one item at a time and re-measure until someone gets to 60 inches exactly.

Shopping Spree

Congratulations! You have just won a $150 shopping spree at a local department store. There are a few rules that you must follow in order to win:

• You may choose only one item in each department.

• You must choose items that, when subtracted from $150, will leave you with $0. No more, and no less.

Get ready to sprint—mathematically. On your mark, get set, GO!

• There are seven different ways to get from $150 to $0 exactly. How many can you find?

Pocket Money

Look in your pocket. Find any loose change?
Four children—James, Kelly, Rachel, and
Pedro—each found five coins in their pockets.
It's up to you to figure out which coins belong to
which child.

Four presidents are shown on the above coins. Do you know who they are?

Read the clues carefully. You may want to take
some notes about your ideas as you go along.

• Pedro spent one coin for a pencil. He then had
60 cents left.

• James put one coin in the box to help the hungry. He then had 60 cents left.

• Rachel found one coin that matched three she
already had. She then had 70 cents.

• Kelly spent one coin on a sticker. She then had
four coins that were alike.

• James and Pedro have exactly the same coins
now. But if Pedro finds a quarter, he'll be back
where he started.

Whose coins are whose?

Gallons of Guppies

Once upon a time there were two guppies, George and Hazel, who lived quite happily in a small fish bowl. Before long, they had babies, and their babies had babies. George and Hazel were a little crowded.

This is where YOU enter the picture. Let's suppose there are 500 guppies in all. It is your job to give them away. You'll give away one guppy on the first day, two guppies on the second day, three guppies on the third day, and so on.

• How many days will it take you to give away all the guppies?

• Will you be able to complete the pattern with your last give-away? (In other words, by following the pattern exactly can you get to 0?)

• Try a different give-away pattern of your own. Describe it. How many days will it take to give away all the guppies? Does following your pattern exactly get you to 0?

And the Answer Is...

Here are some tricks sure to make your friends and family stop and wonder if you have magical powers. So drum up an audience, and let the show begin!

• Write the numbers 198 and 3087 on separate pieces of paper and fold them. Give them to different people to hold. (No peeking.) Now, here's the hard part. Remember who has which answer!

$$\begin{array}{r} 876 \\ -\ 678 \\ \hline 198 \end{array}$$

• Ask someone to give you any three-digit number, such as 543 or 876, in which the digits are consecutive from high to low.

• Have them watch as you reverse the number (so that it reads from low to high) and subtract it from the number they gave you. You may want to use a calculator here.

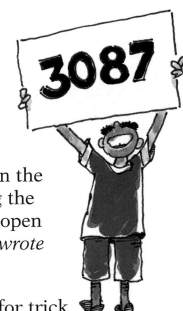

• Ask your audience to read the number in the display. Then point to the person holding the paper with 198 written on it. Have them open the paper and read the answer—*that you wrote down before you even started.*

Now your audience is warmed up. Time for trick number two.

• Ask someone to give you a four-digit number in which the digits are consecutive from high to low.

• Have the crowd watch as you reverse the digits and subtract that number from the first number.

$$
\begin{array}{r}
5432 \\
-\ 2345 \\
\hline
3087
\end{array}
$$

• Once again, show the display. Ask the person with the remaining piece of paper to open it and read the answer.

Take a big bow to the thunderous applause of your audience.

Code Breaking

People have been using codes to send secret messages for almost as long as there has been written language. The Arabs developed a code system more than 1,200 years ago. In Europe, codes first became popular about 600 years ago. They were used by governments to send secret instructions and reports to their representatives in other countries.

And as long as there have been codes, there have been code breakers. Here is your chance to break a code. You will need a calculator.

To read a word, turn your calculator upside down.

• Look at the secret message on the next page. See how many words are missing? Your job is to figure out those words.

• Each missing word is represented by a subtraction problem. Enter the problem on your calculator. The answer that is displayed will spell out the missing word.

• On a separate piece of paper, write down each word as you discover it.

• When you have figured out all the words, you are ready to break the code. What does the message say?

$$\begin{array}{r}8964\\-1246\\\hline\end{array}$$

Dear

$$\begin{array}{r}5926\\-2419\\\hline\end{array}$$

Quick! There is no time to

$$\begin{array}{r}46785\\-11778\\\hline\end{array}\quad\begin{array}{r}721\\-114\\\hline\end{array}$$

Put the map under

$$\begin{array}{r}8231\\-517\\\hline\end{array}\qquad\begin{array}{r}7491\\-2185\\\hline\end{array}$$

on the   . If all   well.

$$\begin{array}{r}543296\\-225759\\\hline\end{array}\qquad\begin{array}{r}9538\\-1803\\\hline\end{array}$$

will pick it up and   it.

$$\begin{array}{r}348\\-347\\\hline\end{array}\quad\begin{array}{r}1136\\-498\\\hline\end{array}$$

you to follow this plan,

$$\begin{array}{r}4762\\-1189\\\hline\end{array}$$

or   !   Good luck,

$$\begin{array}{r}1204\\-396\\\hline\end{array}$$

A-Maze-ing 10,000

Here's a maze to tax your brain cells. Don't use a calculator!

• Put a piece of thin paper over the maze so that you can read the numbers and see the lines through it.

• Begin at 10,000. Try to find a path that will get you to zero exactly.

• Trace your path. Do all the subtraction in your head as you go along. You may not retrace your path along a line. And remember, if at first you don't succeed,.... You know. There may be more than one correct path.

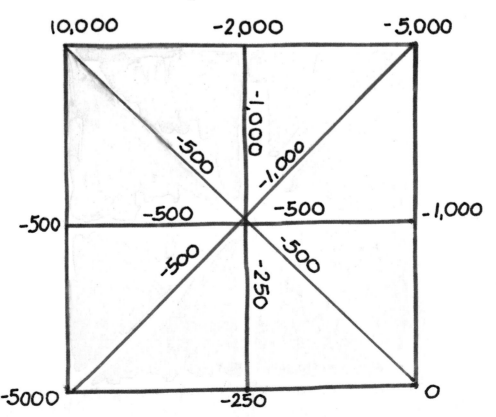

Answers

P. 4, Popcorn Pitch

If you are getting all of the popcorn in the bag every time, you're standing too close. If you aren't getting any in, you're standing too far away. If one of your predictions is wrong, check between the bag and the wall; maybe a piece of popcorn got stuck. If your prediction is still wrong, line up fifteen pieces of popcorn and then take away the number that missed the bag. What's left should be the number you found in the bag.

P. 5, Card Smart

In the first set of hands, the hearts' sum is 15; take away the 8 and you have a remainder of 7. The diamonds' sum is 17; take away the 10 and you have a remainder of 7. The clubs' sum is 12; take away the 5 and you have a remainder of 7. The spades' sum is 14; take away the 7 and you have a remainder of 7.

In the second set of hands, the hearts' sum is 18; take away the 9 and you have a remainder of 9. The diamonds' sum is 12; take away the 3 and you have a remainder of 9. The clubs' sum is 14; take away the 5 and you have a remainder of 9.

Did you come up with a spades hand? Here's one possibility. There are many others.

Pps. 6–7, Checkers Challenge

Red is ahead. Red has 10 pieces left on the board and Black has 8; Red is 2 ahead of Black. You could find this out by covering up a Black and Red piece until you run out of Black pieces; the board would then show how many more Red checkers there are than Black: 2.

Answers

Whenever you find "how many are left?" you use subtraction. In this case, you can start with 12 checkers (the number each player had at the beginning of the game) and take away the number of Red checkers in the pile (5). Using coins or checkers to act this out, you can see that Red has to have 7 checkers left on the board.

In the same way, you can find that Black has only 5 checkers left on the board (12 take away 7).

You can write equations to show what we have done:

$$\begin{array}{r} 12 \\ -5 \\ \hline 7 \end{array} \qquad \text{and} \qquad \begin{array}{r} 12 \\ -7 \\ \hline 5 \end{array}$$

Whenever you compare two numbers, as you do when you find "how many more?" you use subtraction, too. To find how many more checkers Red has than Black, you can subtract the number of checkers still on the board (which you figured out already). Using the numbers we found in the equations above, we could write that equation in this way:

$$7 - 5 = 2$$

You could also find how many more checkers Red has left than Black by comparing the number of checkers that have been taken. If you wrote that equation, it would look like this:

28
$$7 - 5 = 2$$

This equation also answers the last subtraction question, "How many more checkers does Black have to take in order to have taken the same number as Red?"

Pps. 8-9, The Gremlin's Gold
No answers.

P. 10, It's Nothing, Really!
You should end up with seven rows that look like this:

17	12	5	15
5	7	10	2
2	3	8	3
1	5	5	1
4	0	4	0
4	4	4	4
0	0	0	0

You will always end up with a row of fours followed by a row of zeroes.

P. 11, Noodle Numbers
The first noodles stand for the numbers 24 and 32.

The problems are as follows:

$$\begin{array}{r} 25 \\ -16 \\ \hline 9 \end{array} \qquad \begin{array}{r} 40 \\ -32 \\ \hline 8 \end{array} \qquad \text{and} \qquad \begin{array}{r} 32 \\ -26 \\ \hline 6 \end{array}$$

Pps. 12–13, The Tortoise, the Hare, and...
1. The cheetah, 70 miles per hour (mph)
2. The lion, 50 mph
3. The coyote, 43 mph
4. The rabbit, 35 mph

5. The giraffe, 32 mph

6. The cat, 30 mph

7. The human, almost 28 mph

8. The pig, 11 mph

9. The chicken, 9 mph

10. The giant tortoise, less than 1 mph

Pps. 14–15, Red Alert

According to the tally, 17 people wore red and 33 people did not; the "No Red" group is larger. To find out how much larger, you can subtract 17 from 33; the difference is 16.

What were the results of your own tally? Do you think your results might have been different if you had chosen a different place to watch and tally? What about a soccer game? A dentist's office?

If you tallied with a friend, did you ever see someone that was wearing both your favorite color and your friend's? What did you do? Why?

Pps. 16–17, Zero to Sixty

Use subtraction to see how much more or less than 60 inches your total lengths are, and to determine how much closer to 60 inches one player is than another.

Pps. 18–19, Shopping Spree

Correct combinations include:

1. $17 jeans, $46 jacket, $24 shoes, and $63 skis

2. $17 jeans, $39 jacket, $24 shoes, and $70 skis

3. $14 jeans, $46 jacket, $24 shoes, and $66 skis

4. $14 jeans, $44 jacket, $29 shoes, and $63 skis

5. $19 jeans, $44 jacket, $24 shoes, and $63 skis

6. $19 jeans, $39 jacket, $29 shoes, and $63 skis

7. $21 jeans, $39 jacket, $24 shoes, and $66 skis

P. 20, Pocket Money

Pedro's Money

Kelly's Money

James's Money

Rachel's Money

Answers

P. 21, Gallons of Guppies

It takes 32 days to give away all the guppies. The pattern is not exact; on the 32nd day, you only have 4 guppies left to give away.

Pps. 22–23, And the Answer Is...

No answers.

Pps. 24–25, Code Breaking

Dear Bill,

Quick! There is no time to lose. Put the map under the loose log on the hill. If all goes well, Leslie will pick it up and sell it. I beg you to follow this plan, or else!

Good luck,

Bob

P. 26, A-Maze-ing 10,000

Follow the arrows to one possible solution to the maze.

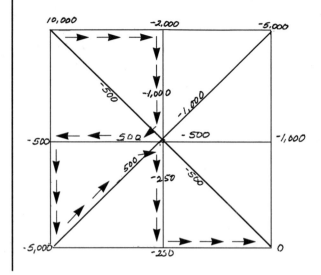

Glossary

difference The amount by which a number is larger or smaller than another, or the amount left when you subtract one number from another.

digit A numeral from 0 to 9.

predict To try and guess the outcome of something.

subtraction The operation in which you find the difference between two numbers; the operation shown by the minus sign; the process in which you take away one number from another.

sum The quantity left when you add together two numbers.

tally To keep or make a count of something.

Index

C
calculator, 22, 24, 26
checkers, 6, 7
code breakers, 24
codes, 24
coins, 6, 8, 20
consecutive digits, 22, 23

D
digits, 22, 23

G
give-away pattern, 21

M
miles per hour, 12–13

N
noodle numbers, 11

R
remainder, 4
row, 10

S
sum, 5
survey, 14, 15

T
tally, 15
tally charts, 14